GREEK ISLAND MYTHS

CHIOS
HOMER

JILL DUDLEY

PUT IT IN YOUR POCKET SERIES
ORPINGTON PUBLISHERS

Published by
Orpington Publishers

Cover design and origination by
Creeds, Bridport, Dorset
01308 423411

Printed and bound in the UK by
Creeds

© Jill Dudley 2016

ISBN: 978-0-9934890-4-4

CHIOS
HOMER

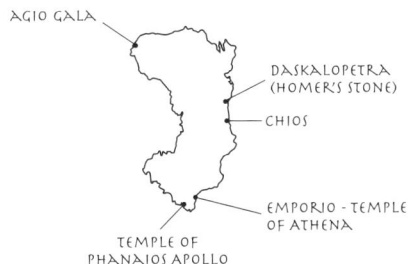

Chios is an east Aegean island, an hour's journey by ferry-boat from Çeşme in Turkey, or about ten hours from Piraeus, the port of Athens. It is forty-eight kilometres long and about twenty wide. A mountain range runs the length of the island from north to south.

Chios claims Homer for its citizen, the blind bard of the eighth or ninth century B.C., from whom the epic poems the *Iliad* and the *Odyssey,* have come down to us. The *Iliad* is inspiring; it is the next best thing to a pagan bible in which gods and men intermingle, emotions run high, and warriors are tested to their limit while divine wills aid their favourite heroes. Homer was the first to give the Olympian gods human form and emotions.

The Greeks did not have writing at the time of Homer,

but the Trojan War had been such a momentous event that the story was spun down the generations verbally, and the stories were depicted on pottery or on other artefacts which kept the memory of it alive.

The *Odyssey* followed on from the *Iliad*, in which Homer sang about the many trials and obstacles which had to be faced, endured and overcome by the great warrior Odysseus* when returning from the Trojan War to his island home of Ithaka. It is full of fabulous tales such as the deadly whirlpool Charybdis, and the multi-headed Scylla to whom Odysseus lost six men. There was also the enchantress Circe who turned Odysseus' companions into pigs; and Calypso whose charm and beauty kept Odysseus with her seven years till the goddess Athena rescued him.

People are divided as to which epic they prefer; some find the *Iliad* too traumatic, preferring the adventures in the *Odyssey*, while others love the heroism of the warriors in the *Iliad* and the intervention of the gods, and find the *Odyssey* too fanciful. Alexander the Great was a great admirer of the *Iliad*, and always carried a copy of it on his campaigns.

In the suburbs of Chios port, at a place called Vrondatos, is the *Daskalopetra*, the Teacher's Stone. A footpath leads up a low hill through fir trees and, on a terrace about fourteen metres square in size, is a low round rocky platform about five metres in diameter. To one side, and rising from it, is a waist-high rough stone, the *Daskalopetra*. It is there that tradition has it Homer taught his pupils; there that he played his lyre and sang his epic poems to an audience seated spellbound on the ground around him. Before the town of Chios spread out from the port itself, the location for Homer's Stone would have been rural and tranquil. Behind it would have been the same lofty, grandiose grey-pink crags which are seen today, and before it the broad sweep of glittering sea with the landmass of Turkey looming on the horizon. A little further along the Turkish coastline would have been where the Greek fleet had once anchored at Beşik bay and the Trojan War battles had been fought out on the Trojan plain.

Homer was popularly known as the 'blind bard'. Yet so many things within his epic poems were vividly described. Regarding Charybdis, the whirlpool, in his *Odyssey*, he wrote: *...she seethed and swirled throughout all her depths like a cauldron set on a great fire, and overhead the spray fell down on the tops of the two rocks. But when she sucked the sea-water in, one might look right down through the swirling eddy while the rock roared hideously around her and the sea-floor came to view, dark and sandy...* (Odyssey 12:235-240)

Could Homer only have known this from other people's descriptions? Or had he never seen for himself what he so vividly described in the *Iliad*, an army camped out at night and waiting for morning: *...they sat along the lines of battle, and many fires burned. As the stars in the sky stand out in all their splendour round the bright moon, when the upper air is still; when every lookout place, headland and mountain ravine stands out, and infinite upper air floods down from the skies; when many were the fires, lit by the Trojans, that could be seen in front of Ilium* (Troy) *between the streams of Scamander and the Greek ships. There were a thousand fires burning on the plain, and round each one sat fifty men in the light of its blaze, while horses stood beside their chariots, munching white barley and rye, and awaiting Dawn on her golden throne...* (Iliad 8:550-563)

The Teacher's Stone is believed by some scholars to be a crude throne of the goddess Cybele, a Phrygian fertility goddess; the claws of a lion can be seen at its base, a customary feature of the thrones of this goddess; the sliver-like polished patches of cream on the rugged creamy-pinky-grey stone suggest it is of ancient marble. If Homer now is silent, today the cicadas sing loud and clear around the site.

In the far south-east of the island is a place called Emporio where a major temple of Athena existed on an acropolis high above the ruins of a settlement below. Before the temple was built there had been an altar dating from the eighth century B.C. Homer might well have come there to honour the goddess who figured so much in both his epic poems. The goddess Athena played a major part in Homer's *Odyssey,* disguising herself and advising Odysseus how best to get home. From the acropolis heights you get a panoramic view down rugged slopes to the island's shoreline of coves and creeks, and to the sapphire-blue sea.

To the far south-west of Chios are the remains of a temple of Apollo Phanaios (Phanaios means 'divine manifestation'). To reach it one must drive several kilometres on a dirt track alongside an ever widening gorge full of olive trees. The ruins are near the mouth of the estuary, and from there the sea can be glimpsed glittering in the distance.

The Phanaios epithet is not because Apollo manifested himself at the site, but because of the long-held belief that his mother Leto, while pregnant, had come there after the goddess Hera, Zeus' wife, enraged at her husband's fling with Leto, had forbidden anywhere on earth to allow her to give birth. It was here that Leto learned that the tiny island of

Delos, till then submerged, would be raised from the seabed for her confinement. The area then became known as the Delos of Chios. It is an atmospheric, isolated spot, and the worship of Apollo there dates back to the ninth century – yet another location that Homer could have visited.

Apollo featured in the *Iliad* on numerous occasions. He supported the Trojans and intervened to get the results he wanted, such as wrapping a Trojan in a thick mist to avoid certain death, or guiding an arrow, or diverting a sword. When his father Zeus tipped the balance in favour of a Greek victory, Apollo had to acquiesce to his authority.

To the far north-west of Chios, on the side of a tree-filled ravine, is the tiny ancient Church of Agio Gala where a small surprise awaits the visitor. The church is visible from the ravine below, nestling against the high rockface, its whitewashed round drum pierced with small arched windows under a terra-cotta tiled roof. Its terrace is reached by flagged steps and the inner part of the church is built into a cave, beyond which is a second cave dedicated to Agia Anna. From there it is possible to enter a third cave with udder-shaped stalactites (called 'mastoid stalactites') from which calciferous water drips resembling breast milk. This is believed to have miraculous healing qualities and is collected in wide bowls placed beneath these 'udders'. It is where the earliest worship in pagan times had taken place.

The small surprise about this location is that, before the nearby village was called Agio Gala, it had been known as Agios Thelenis or Agia Eleni. Long before Christianity, local tradition had it that Helen of Troy* had visited the island and was worshipped there as a goddess. Due to Aphrodite's wiles

Helen had run off with King Priam of Troy's son Paris which resulted in the Trojan War. It might well be that Homer knew of the worship of Helen as a goddess in this area, and it was that which inspired him with his *Iliad*.

Chios is full of grandeur and beauty with dramatic mountains, and tranquil coves. It is inspirational and unique, which is surely why Homer drew from it the drama of his two world renowned epic poems, the *Iliad* and the *Odyssey*. In both, human strength, courage and endurance play their part.

It requires time and trouble to get to Chios, but then the best things often are the ones that need effort and determination. Once there no visitor can fail to be affected by its idyllic charm, or to feel regret when he finally leaves.

* Denotes a separate booklet on the subject.

THE IMMORTAL GODS BORN OF ZEUS BY MORTAL WOMEN

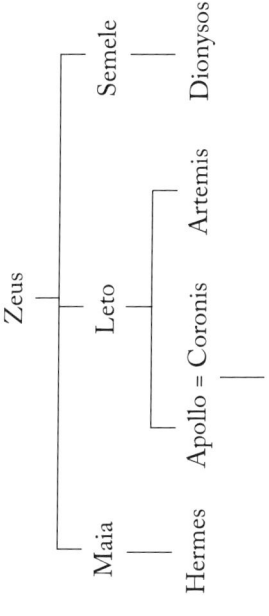

GODDESS ATHENA'S FAMILY TREE

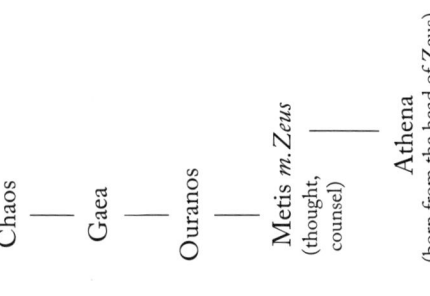

Chaos — Gaea — Ouranos — Metis *m. Zeus*
(thought, counsel)
|
Athena
(born from the head of Zeus)

GLOSSARY OF GODS AND GODDESSES

APOLLO – Son of Zeus and Leto, and twin brother of Artemis. He was god of music, archery and prophecy. In the Trojan War he supported the Trojans.

APHRODITE – Goddess of love. In the Trojan War she supported the Trojans.

ATHENA – Daughter of Zeus. She was born mature and fully armed from his head. She was goddess of handicraft, and was protectress of many cities, but especially Athens. She was the embodiment of wisdom, and in the Trojan War she supported the Greeks.

CYBELE – Originally a Phrygian goddess. She was often identified with Rhea, the mother of Zeus and Hera and other major Greek gods and goddesses. She was the embodiment of Mother Earth, and a fertility goddess.

HELEN – Semi-divine. Her mortal father was King Tyndareus of Sparta, but Zeus, supreme god of the ancient world, seduced Leda, her mother, taking the shape of a swan for his love-making. It was Helen, the most beautiful woman in the world, who ran off with Paris, son of King Priam of Troy, which caused the Trojan War.

HERA – Wife of Zeus. She was goddess of women and marriage.

LEDA – Wife of King Tyndareus of Sparta, and mother of Helen.

TITANS – The offspring of Ouranos (often spelt Uranus, the heavens) and Gaea (the earth). There were said to be twelve of them, six sons and six daughters. Kronos was one of the sons, and Rhea one of the daughters. These two gave birth to Zeus, Hera and several other of the Olympian gods.

ZEUS – Son of Kronos and Rhea. God of the heavens, and supreme god of the ancient world having deposed his father.

ACKNOWLEDGEMENT

Grateful acknowledgement to Richmond Lattimore's translation of
Homer's *The Iliad,* the University of Chicago Press, published 2011.
Also to Richmond Lattimore's translation of *The Odyssey,*
Harper Perennial Modern Classics edition, published 2007.

MORE FROM THE
PUT IT IN YOUR POCKET SERIES
GREEK MYTHS

TROJAN WAR
THE JUDGEMENT OF PARIS
HELEN
KING AGAMEMNON
ACHILLES
THE WOODEN HORSE
ODYSSEUS

SACRED SITES
ATHENS – THE ACROPOLIS
CORINTH – ST. PAUL AND THE GODDESS OF LOVE
DELPHI – THE ORACLE OF APOLLO
ELEUSIS – DEMETER AND KORE
EPIDAURUS – CENTRE OF HEALING
OLYMPIA – THE OLYMPIC GAMES

ALSO BY JILL DUDLEY

YE GODS! (TRAVELS IN GREECE)
YE GODS! II (MORE TRAVELS IN GREECE)
LAP OF THE GODS (TRAVELS IN CRETE
AND THE AEGEAN ISLANDS)